I Have the Right to
Save My Planet

Published in English in Canada and the USA in 2021 by
Groundwood Books
First published in French in 2019 as *J'ai le droit de sauver ma
planète* by Rue du Monde
Copyright © 2019 by Rue du Monde
English translation copyright © 2021 by Groundwood Books

Groundwood Books / House of Anansi Press
groundwoodbooks.com

Groundwood Books respectfully acknowledges that the land on
which we operate is the Traditional Territory of many Nations,
including the Anishinabeg, the Wendat and the Haudenosaunee. It
is also the Treaty Lands of the Mississaugas of the Credit.

We gratefully acknowledge the Government of Canada for its
financial support of our publishing program.

With the participation of the Government of Canada
Avec la participation du gouvernement du Canada | Canadä

Library and Archives Canada Cataloguing in Publication
Title: I have the right to save my planet / Alain Serres ; pictures by
Aurélia Fronty.
Other titles: J'ai le droit de sauver ma planète. English
Names: Serres, Alain, author. | Fronty, Aurélia, illustrator. | Tanaka,
Shelley, translator.
Description: Translation of: J'ai le droit de sauver ma planète. |
Translated by Shelley Tanaka.
Identifiers: Canadiana (print) 20200276352 | Canadiana (ebook)
20200276360 | ISBN 9781773064871 (hardcover) | ISBN
9781773064888 (EPUB) | ISBN 9781773064895 (Kindle)
Subjects: LCSH: Children's rights—Juvenile literature. |
LCSH: Children and the environment—Juvenile literature. |
LCSH: Sustainable development—Juvenile literature. | LCSH:
Environmental protection—Juvenile literature.
Classification: LCC HQ789 .S47 2021 | DDC j323.3/52—dc23

The illustrations were rendered in gouache.
Printed and bound in Malaysia

I Have the Right to Save My Planet

Words by
Alain Serres

Pictures by
Aurélia Fronty

Translated by
Shelley Tanaka

GROUNDWOOD BOOKS
HOUSE OF ANANSI PRESS
TORONTO / BERKELEY

Everything here is free!
The sun and its rays of light are free. The chirping of the birds, the shade
beneath the trees, the golden dandelions — all free.
It's not like going to the store, where you have to pay for everything.

**When it comes to nature,
I have the right
to everything.**

What about the air?
It's for the land and people everywhere!
And the green grass?
Free for the cows!
And all that good cow dung?
A gift for all the flies in the sky!

When we come into the world, it gives us a huge gift — its birds, trees, mammals, corals, microscopic animals, flowers, insects, fish, bacteria, mushrooms ... **More than ten million species live with us on this planet ...** And we're discovering fifty new species each day.

In the forests of New Guinea, researchers have found a tiny frog with a pointy nose that can stick straight out. They've named it *Litoria pinocchio* — the Pinocchio treefrog.

I have the right to cheer, "Hurray for diversity!"

(But not too loud. Don't want to wake up the frog baby.)

Come on, humans! Time to wake up!
Scientists are warning us that many species will
disappear if we continue to mistreat nature.
Plenty of them have disappeared already.

I have the right to know that in Borneo,
people are destroying rainforests to make
room for palm trees.
Why? Because oil from the palm fruit is an
inexpensive ingredient used to make some
cookies, margarine and shower gels.

I have the right to know that by clearing the rainforest, humans are dangerously reducing the habitat of the great apes.

Without enough food and shelter, some of them, like the orangutans, could disappear forever.

I have the right to say, "I don't want the rainforest to be replaced with palm trees. I don't want those cookies, not even the chocolate ones."

13

Scientists who study the natural world are warning us that
the Earth could lose
one million plant and animal species
if we don't take more care —
from the tigers in Sumatra to the ibex in the Alps, from the
white orchids of Kenya to the manatees in the Caribbean.

**These animals and plants need us to protect them and the
places where they live.**

Each species depends on the others.
So if a plant disappears, the insects that feed on its flowers
will vanish, too.
And so will the frogs that eat those insects, and the fish that
feed on the eggs of those frogs ...

**The great chain of life goes all the way around
the planet.
We must not interrupt it.**

I know all this, so I have the right to take action.

To grow plants that will
attract bees.

To preserve the places where
birds and insects live.

To get together with my friends and make posters to save the leatherback sea turtle.

To send a message to the leaders of the world, signed by my whole family, saying, "Help protect our planet."

I even have the right to go out and demonstrate with my parents.

I have the right to do all this because I'm a child. Because it's written down in the Convention on the Rights of the Child.

But most of all, because I love life!

Water is the source of life, and all life depends on it. The Earth is like a giant drop of water — in our lakes, rivers, oceans, clouds, rain and underground aquifers.

Ever since the planet was formed, water has been the most valuable resource for all of us — humans, plants and animals.

There is no more water available than what we have now — not even a tiny drop.

It's up to us humans to take care of this water.

We are the only ones who know that even though there is a lot of saltwater on the planet, the fresh water that we drink is extremely rare.

And we are the only ones who know not to pollute or waste the most precious liquid in the world.

Even if I'm poor, I have the right to water.
Even if I live in the desert,
I have the right to expect that my neighbors on
the other side of the world will join hands to help
me find the drinking water that I need.

As for me, I will share with them the stories
of the place where I live.

Then they can share my stories with each other by the lakes in their country, where water flows freely. And together, even far away from each other, we can all dream of the day when the Earth will be saved.

Because we will protect our planet well and share what we have.

"Oh, no! Don't do that!"

I have the right to yell at my parents if they throw a plastic bottle into a stream. Because that bottle will never disappear.

Not in the stream, or in the river, or in the waves that wash up in the harbor, or in the deep and vast ocean.

A bottle, transparent as a shrimp, that a whale might swallow.
And that whale may get sick because it already has a belly full of
plastic trash.

I can also decide

that in my family we will buy less plastic,
and in the grocery store we will choose the packaging
that is the cleanest and safest for nature.

I have the right to ask that we no longer make plastic straws, plastic bags or plastic containers that we don't know how to recycle.

I even have the right to imagine a machine that makes *flastic*.
It would be like plastic, but made with flowers!
And when you throw it out, it becomes good soil that helps new flowers grow.

Long live the imagination and toys made out of flowers for all the children in the world!

It takes hard work to change all our bad habits.

I need to build up my strength by eating apples, carrots and beans. **But I have the right to prefer fruits and vegetables that are grown without pesticides or chemical fertilizers.**

These things are bad for our health.

These chemicals are as dangerous for humans as they are for animals — even fish, which absorb them after the rains and rivers have carried them into the ocean.

But I have the right to think that one day
soon,
farmers will no longer use chemicals. They will
choose other ways to grow better crops.

**And the soil will get healthy
again, and the land will come
back to life.**

I also have the right to hope that
tomorrow,
humans will learn to share the energy of each grain of rice
and the smile of every watermelon.
And not a single child on Earth will ever go hungry again.

When I look up at the sky and the sun, I ask
myself all kinds of questions.

Why is the planet getting warmer and warmer?
Why are forests burning, and why is ice melting
right under the feet of polar bears?

And why does it rain way too much in some places,
until floods wash away houses and rivers overflow and
drown the land?

I have the right to know the truth.
It isn't the sky or the sun that is the problem.
It's humans!

We are experiencing climate change because there are more and more factories, cars, trucks and planes on the planet.
When they consume oil to run their engines, they produce carbon dioxide, a gas that is not harmful in small quantities ...

But if there's too much of it, this carbon dioxide becomes dangerous for all living things.
What's more, it holds the sun's heat all around the Earth, as if we were shut inside a gigantic greenhouse.

Luckily, trees are able to absorb a lot of carbon dioxide.

So why would we ever let our forests disappear?

Oh, and I have the right to come up with a great idea right now!

What if, one day, all the children in the world walked out of their
schools dressed as polar bears?
I mean, *all* the children — in China, South Africa,
Argentina, France, Australia ...

Bears everywhere. Even the teachers would be bears, angry about all the human activities that are damaging the planet.

And all together, we would cry,

GRRRRRRRF

RRRRROUAAAAAH !

Maybe everyone in the world would hear us.

Then maybe all those people stuck in traffic on the highway would decide to take a train that produces less carbon dioxide than a thousand cars.

Maybe the destroyers of the forests would become gardeners instead.

Or maybe a child would dare to invent the Zero Emission Airplane, which would use the energy of the sun and the wind.

And I even have the right to dream that this
child inventor who saves the planet is me!

But look, don't count on me to be the only superhero
who saves the planet.
Everyone has to do their part.

If the three billion kids in the world found three billion good ideas, the planet would grow more beautiful every day. But don't forget! Before they can take good care of the planet, children must not live in poverty.

They must be in good health, be able to go to school, be respected and listened to. Otherwise they will only be able to think about their problems.

The world's children have an international convention on their rights.

It was invented to protect them from all the things that can spoil their lives, the way feathers protect birds from the rain.

By signing this agreement, almost all the world's leaders have declared,
"A child's best interests must always be respected. That matters more than anything else."

I have the right to say,
"So, that also means respecting the child's magnificent home — the Earth!"

41

Respect the corner of the planet where each child lives. Respect the water we drink, the air we breathe. The fruit we eat, the sparrow whose song makes us smile.

Respect our countryside, our rivers, our oceans — including the ones we may never see. Even if they are far away, they belong to all children, too.

Respect our extended family — all of humanity and our one trillion cousins, the plants and animals, whether huge or almost invisible.

This would be the greatest gift for each small earthling —

that humans will take care of our planet as if it were their very own child.

Also in the series:

I Have the Right to Be a Child

An IRA Notable Book for a Global Society
A Children's Literature Assembly Notable Children's Book
A USBBY Outstanding International Book

In the first book in the series, a young narrator describes what it means to be a child with rights — from the right to food, water and shelter, to the right to go to school, to be free from violence, to breathe clean air, and more. The book emphasizes that these rights belong to every child on the planet, whether they are "black or white, small or big, rich or poor, born here or somewhere else."

Hardcover with jacket • ISBN 978-1-55498-149-6
EPUB • 978-1-55498-208-0

★ "Provocative and guaranteed to spark awareness of children's rights."
— *Kirkus*, starred review

"[A] powerful work, and a handsome one." — *Publishers Weekly*

I Have the Right to Culture

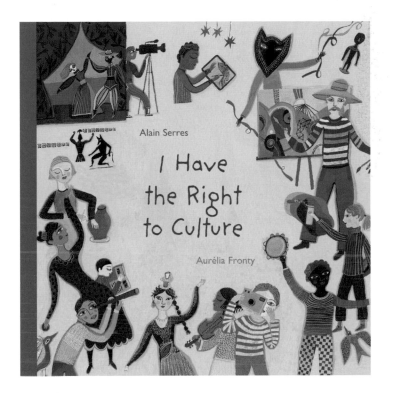

Publishing Fall 2021

From the author and illustrator duo who created the award-winning *I Have the Right to Be a Child* and *I Have the Right to Save My Planet* comes this beautifully illustrated third book in the series. *I Have the Right to Culture* explores a child's right to be curious, and to experience all of humanity's shared knowledge, including music, art, dance and much more.

Hardcover with jacket • ISBN 978-1-77306-490-1
EPUB • 978-1-77306-491-8